JAMES

SIMPLY THE GOSPEL

Other studies in the Not Your Average Bible Study series

Ruth

Psalms

Jonah

Malachi

Sermon on the Mount

Ephesians

Colossians

Hebrews

1 Peter

2 Peter and Jude

1–3 John

For updates on this series, visit lexhampress.com/nyab

JAMES

SIMPLY THE GOSPEL

NOT YOUR AVERAGE BIBLE STUDY

JOHN D. BARRY

James: Simply the Gospel
Not Your Average Bible Study

Copyright 2014 Lexham Press

Lexham Press, 1313 Commercial St., Bellingham, WA 98225
LexhamPress.com

ISBN 978-1-57-799550-0

Academic Editor: Michael S. Heiser
Managing Editor: Rebecca Van Noord
Assistant Editors: Jessi Strong, Joel Wilcox
Cover Design: Christine Gerhart
Typesetting: projectluz.com

CONTENTS

HOW TO USE
THIS RESOURCE

Not Your Average Bible Study is a series of in-depth Bible studies that can be used for individual or group study. Depending on your individual needs or your group pace, you may opt to cover one lesson a week or more.

Each lesson prompts you to dig deep into the Word—as such, we recommend you use your preferred translation with this study. The author used his own translation, but included quotations from the English Standard Version. Whatever Bible version you use, please be sure you leave ample time to get into the Bible itself.

To assist you, we recommend using the Faithlife Study Bible, which is also edited by John D. Barry. You can download this digital resource for free for your tablet, phone, personal computer, or use it online. Go to FaithlifeBible.com to learn more.

May God bless you in the study of His Word.

INTRODUCTION

Many of us have fallen victim to the notion that life is just a series of pursuits. We get caught up in the details at the cost of the big picture. It can be difficult and frustrating to be told that the gospel is simple when life seems complicated.

James helps us look at our lives with a new perspective. He questions everything that we think matters, to show us what is really important: simply the gospel—lived through how we think, feel and act.

PART I: SELF-EXAMINATION

JAMES 1

Nostalgia is a result of a desire for simpler times. When everything changes for us, it's no surprise that we feel disoriented and want things to be the way they were. The book of James, though, says that when we "encounter various trials," we learn what it means to be whole, complete and perfected by God.

Perfection seems like a distant idea. We have no problem acknowledging that no one will achieve it. Yet the things that most people believe *can* be achieved, such as fulfillment in wealth, are actually impossible. Perhaps the profundity of perfection is the exact reason why James calls us to self-examination.

EXPERIENCING GOD'S WORD

Pray that the Holy Spirit would make the letter of James easy for you to understand.

Read the entire letter of James aloud in one sitting.

This letter was likely circulated and read aloud in front of various church congregations. Reading it aloud helps us to experience it like the original audience would have. As you read, underline what you consider the key words (or points of emphasis) and the words "let," "now," "therefore," "but," "if" and "like"—these words signal when James is presenting a new idea or contrast. What are the major themes and big ideas?

_____

_____

_____

What are some ways that James wants you to approach life differently?

_____

_____

_____

What are four ideas James presents that, if incorporated into your life, could dramatically change the way you approach others and God? Contemplate those. Ask the Spirit to help you understand how God wants to use those ideas to work in your life.

_____

_____

_____

ENDURANCE IS A VIRTUE

Pray that God would show you what He desires to teach you through trials.

Read the entire book of James again. Reflect on verses 1:1-4.

Repeatedly reading a biblical book helps us internalize its words, allowing for the Bible's message to come to us in times of need.

James emphasized the phrase "of God and of the Lord Jesus Christ" in the original Greek, signaling that his relationship to God—as a person under the authority of Jesus, the anointed one—is the most important thing to him. He calls himself a "slave" of Christ to further indicate his subservient relationship: Christ is in charge of his life. How would you describe your relationship to Christ? Does it match or contradict this description? If it contradicts it, how can you change that?

_____

_____

_____

_____

_____

The author identifies his audience as "the 12 tribes in the dispersion"—the Jewish people scattered across the known world of the first century. As a people group with no country, Jewish people shared a religious, ethnic and cultural heritage, which they took pride in and were persecuted for. Jewish Christians were oppressed both as Jews and Christians by the Roman government since their ethnicity and many of their practices remained the same, in spite of their new identity in Christ. They were often condemned by fellow Jews as well for their conversion. To be a Christian in this time was beyond inconvenient; it was painful. It always involved being willing to sacrifice everything, including your family, job and even your life.

James calls his audience "my brothers" (which by extension also means "my sisters"), indicating that he views them as family because of their similar relationship to Christ (1:2). Why does James say that we should "count it all joy" when we "encounter various trials" (1:2–3)?

_____

_____

_____

How will endurance affect us (1:4)? By way of analogy, think about what athletes encounter when they train.

_____

_____

_____

What trials are you experiencing? How do you think God would like you to respond?

_____

_____

_____

BECOMING WISE

Pray that God would help you to gain wisdom.

Read James 1:1–27. Reflect on verses 1:5–8.

Reading each section of Scripture in its larger context helps us to understand the author's main argument.

What does 1:5 tell us we should seek when we experience "trials" (1:2)? How can we obtain this (1:6)?

_____

_____

_____

_____

How does God react when we ask for wisdom? What will happen after we ask for it (1:5)?

_____

_____

_____

Doubt in 1:6 is juxtaposed against faith—making faith the antidote for doubt. Faith here is not an abstract concept or specific persuasion; it is being subservient to Christ, like James is (1:1). What happens to the person who doubts (1:6)? What is a person who doubts like (1:8)?

_____

_____

_____

Are you more like the person with faith or the person with doubt?

_____

_____

_____

Overcoming doubt means gaining discernment, which is essentially wisdom. Discernment can help us navigate any difficulty. What do you need to give to Christ in order to overcome the doubt in your life? What are you attempting to rule that you should let Christ rule instead?

_____

_____

_____

BOASTING ABOUT THE RIGHT THINGS

Pray that Christ would teach you what's worth boasting about.

Read James 1:1–11. Reflect on verses 1:9–11.

Who does James say should "boast," and why (1:9)? What does the author want to see happen (1:10)? The point of this passage is not that wealth itself is an evil thing, but that wealth used for the wrong purposes—which is usually the case, even unknowingly—is evil.

_____

_____

_____

Read Isaiah 40:6. What does the grass in James 1:10–11 represent (also compare 1 Pet 1:24)?

_____

_____

_____

The flower represents wealth or the wealthy man, standing alone. What does this parallelism indicate about the very notion of wealth? Where do those who make it their priority ultimately end up?

_____

_____

_____

Are the person who pursues wealth and the person who doubts similar (Jas 1:8, 11)? In light of this, what priorities in your life need to change?

_____

_____

_____

TEMPTATION DOESN'T DESERVE ITS PLACE

Pray that the Spirit would help you fight the evil in your life.

Read James 1:1–15. Reflect on verses 1:12–15.

In 1:12, James ties his discussion together. What are the problems he has addressed leading up to this verse?

_____

_____

_____

What happens when we endure trials for the sake of Christ (1:12)? This verse does not support faith based upon our actions; instead, it proposes that we love God. Because we love God, we choose to act on our faith and endure when things get difficult.

_____

_____

_____

_____

How are we tempted (1:13–14)? Who can we blame for our failures?

_____

_____

_____

_____

What happens when we give in to our own desires (1:15)? How do our desires relate to the problems that James has already addressed?

_____

_____

_____

_____

In contrast to temptation and sin, what produces good things (1:2–4)?

_____

_____

_____

We have a say in the progression of events in our lives—it all has to do with the doors we open and the ones we close. Overcoming sin happens when we choose not to open the doors that lead to it; hence Jesus tells us to pray, "lead us not into temptation" (Matt 6:13). We must choose the path that keeps us away from sin and leads us toward faith.

Think about your major failings. What actions could you change that would prevent you from sinning?

_____

_____

_____

_____

ORDER OUT OF CHAOS

Pray that God would help you to gain discernment.

Read James 1:1–18. Reflect on verses 1:16–18.

Discerning right from wrong is not always easy. When moral dilemmas present themselves, though, Jas 1:16–17 offers an answer. Where does the right choice, the "good gift," come from (1:17)? Why is this gift perfect?

_____

_____

_____

_____

Read 1 John 1:5. What does the phrase "Father of lights" mean (Jas 1:17)?

_____

_____

_____

_____

Who are we to God (1:18)? Why do we matter? (See Genesis 2 and Romans 1:19–23.)

_____

_____

_____

_____

Jewish people in this time thought of themselves as God's "firstfruits"—the best and first part of His creation. This view was correct (Jer 2:3; Mal 3:6) until Jesus came and radically changed everything. All people who believe in Christ are now part of His family (Rom 8:23). By extension, all believers who remain steadfast are the firstfruits (Rev 14:4) of God's creation—they are the beginning of God's new creation on earth (2 Cor 5:17). Believers are a sign of God's work among humanity and His desire to bring order to our chaotic world as He did in the beginning.

How does God want to use you to bring order to our chaotic world? What is your part in His plan? What part do God's "gift" and the discernment He gives you play in this?

_____

_____

_____

_____

BEING WHO WE WERE MADE TO BE

Pray that Christ would show you an accurate picture of what you are meant to be.

Read James 1:1–25. Reflect on verses 1:19–25.

What are the three things that we should do, according to 1:19? How are these instructions connected to James' thoughts on wisdom (1:5–7)?

_____

_____

_____

James 1:20 implies that anger keeps us from acting according to God's standards. How can we "put away all moral uncleanness and wicked excess" (1:21)? According to 1:10 and 1:14, what excesses does James have in view?

_____

_____

_____

What can "save our souls" (1:21)? Read John 1:1–5. Who embodies this idea? Who should we accept and seek?

_____

_____

_____

_____

When we accept God's desires for our lives, how should we begin to act (Jas 1:22)? What happens to us when we do not act this way (1:23-24)?

_____

_____

_____

Read Hebrews 10:15-18. According to Hebrews—and Jeremiah 31:33, which the author of Hebrews is quoting—where does the "law" reside?

_____

_____

_____

What happens when we follow God's will (Jas 1:25)?

_____

_____

_____

What sort of person does Christ want you to be? How is this different from the way you are currently living?

_____

_____

_____

What can you do differently this week that will change your focus and remind you of Christ's work in your life?

_____

_____

_____

TRUE RELIGION

Pray that God would teach you what true religion is about.

Read James 1:1–27. Reflect on verses 1:26–27.

What happens when we aren't careful about what we say (1:26)? What can our actions nullify? What can our actions do to us, as well as others?

_____

_____

_____

Rather than focusing on what we shouldn't do, 1:27 tells us what we *should* do; it seems the adage "staying busy keeps you out of trouble" is biblically sound. If we stay busy doing the right things, the wrong things are usually kept at bay. What right things does James suggest (1:27)? What is the result of that work?

_____

_____

_____

Do you currently act in the way that James instructs? Are you concerned about those who have the least and need the most? Are you doing something about it? If not, think of ways you can and start acting upon those ideas. Perhaps the cure to the ailments of sin, pain and frustration in your life is simply spending more time caring for those who are hurting.

_____

_____

_____

CONCLUSION

If religion is about practicing one thing, our religion should be about being like Christ. We are called to live according to His desires; we must be led by our relationship with Him. Our lives, and those of others, will continue to be in shambles until we begin to live for the purpose of helping and loving other people. It's such a simple idea, which is precisely why it's part of Christ's gospel.

JAMES 2

At times, faith becomes a convenience store: We get what we want, when we want it, and when satisfied, we ignore the rest. We'll return again, at our own convenience, and when we do, we will be partial to certain spiritual products that satisfy our particular desires. What we want is what we will have.

Faith is marketed, bought and sold at the low price of listening in a church building for an hour. Usually, participation is optional; after all, God meets us where we are, and He hopes we will be thankful and come again. Although both statements are technically true, they are insufficient slogans.

For this reason, James opposes partiality and abstract faith. His brand of faith is more difficult, yet more fulfilling, than what's marketed today. In these next eight studies, we will relearn the simple gospel.

DEFINING FAITH

Pray that the Holy Spirit would make God's word clear.

Read the entire letter of James aloud in one sitting, slowly.

Reading aloud helps us remember and ponder God's Word. It provides us with the opportunity to meditate upon God's Word (Psa 1).

As you read, double underline the key words "my brothers," "faith," "works" and "blessed." These words introduce the prominent thoughts and themes of the book. Also, put a square around each question mark. James regularly asks rhetorical questions that should be understood as principles. For example, when he says "Did not God choose the poor of the world to be rich in faith, and heirs of the kingdom that he has promised to those who love him?" (2:5), he means: "God chose the poor to be rich in faith—they will inherit His kingdom." James himself emphasizes this when he follows his rhetorical question with, "But you have dishonored the poor!" (2:6).

What are the major themes of James?

_____

_____

_____

_____

Based on the letter of James, how would you define faith? How should your actions change to fit this definition?

_____

_____

_____

_____

IMPARTIAL FAITH

Pray that God would show you how your interactions with others can be improved.

Read James 1:1–2:26. Reflect on verses 2:1–4.

What titles does James apply to Jesus (2:1)? The word "Lord" is about authority—being a ruling power. "Christ" means "anointed one," or God's chosen. What effect does James' definition have on our faith?

_____

_____

_____

In what ways do you show partiality (2:1)? Do you or others in your church community show partiality in the ways that James describes (2:2–3)?

_____

_____

_____

_____

What does James think of these decisions toward partiality (2:4)? What do these decisions show us about our character?

_____

_____

_____

_____

Why should we refrain from being "judges" (2:4; see John 5:30)? How do you feel when someone judges you? How do you respond?

_____

_____

_____

How can you change your actions to better align them with God's view?

_____

_____

_____

HEIRS OF THE KINGDOM

Pray that God would show you what it means to be rich in faith.

Read James 2:1–7. Reflect on verses 2:5–7.

Who did God choose to be "rich in faith" (2:5)?

_____

_____

_____

_____

The book of James often reflects Jesus' sermon in Luke 6:17–49. In light of Luke 6:20–21, what is the context and overall message of James 2:5–6?

_____

_____

_____

_____

James 2:6 reflects Luke 6:24–26, as well as the situation of Christ-believers at the time. The ruling class was persecuting James' readers for their beliefs. What does James say about the rich (2:7)? Why is it wrong to favor them, even if they provide funding for the church?

_____

_____

_____

_____

James' message goes beyond treating all people as equal. Indeed, Christ has made all equal (Gal 3:28), but that's only one level of James' message. For James, our treatment of the poor is connected to our relationship with Christ, as well as the message we send about Him to other people. The gospel is more than just ideas; it's really actions and choices.

What are the social ramifications of the church acting differently than the typical company or nonprofit? How does it change our approach to ministry? In what ways do you need to change your approach to ministry?

_____

_____

_____

LIFE, LIBERTY AND THE PURSUIT OF CHRIST

Pray that Christ would reveal how you can be more diligent about following Him.

Read James 2:1–13. Reflect on verses 2:8–13.

What one thing can we do (the "royal law") that will alter the rest of our actions (2:8)? How is this law both simple and complex, and what happens when we fail to keep it (2:9–10)? The two Old Testament laws that James lists in 2:11 reflect the basic premise of the law in 2:8.

_____

_____

_____

_____

While we should uphold the royal law, by what law should we ultimately live (2:12)?

_____

_____

_____

_____

Living by the "law of liberty" means acting on our faith (1:22–25). The law of liberty is faith in Christ (2:1) coupled with the actions that faith requires (2:12). Liberty doesn't result in the freedom to be lawless (immoral); it results in being lawful according to the values and virtues of the Holy Spirit. We are blessed when we do what God has asked of us (1:25).

In what ways is judgment, based upon Old Testament law, without mercy? How does mercy triumph over judgment (2:13)?

_____

_____

_____

Based on this, what do you need to do differently? How is your view of faith skewed, and how does it need to be corrected?

_____

_____

_____

Write down three ways that your faith doesn't align with James' view, then identify practical ways to change.

_____

_____

_____

ACTION ITEMS

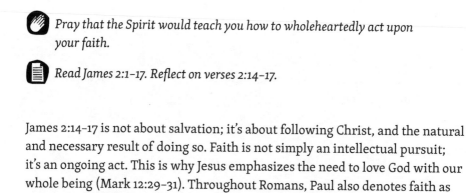

Pray that the Spirit would teach you how to wholeheartedly act upon your faith.

Read James 2:1–17. Reflect on verses 2:14–17.

James 2:14–17 is not about salvation; it's about following Christ, and the natural and necessary result of doing so. Faith is not simply an intellectual pursuit; it's an ongoing act. This is why Jesus emphasizes the need to love God with our whole being (Mark 12:29–31). Throughout Romans, Paul also denotes faith as something that requires action. Paul and James both agree that the Law can be set aside in favor of following Christ wholeheartedly (see week 12; compare Rom 3:20, 28; Gal 3:10–11).

Similarly, John's Gospel, which notes that salvation comes to all who have faith (John 3:16–17), regularly emphasizes the need for the disciples to act on their faith—through both difficult circumstances and hardships. James' point in 2:14 is that faith without works is actually not faith at all (2:14). Faith is connected to actions: When we believe in something, we act upon that belief. Otherwise, we are merely intellectually, not physically, engaged.

You may not have ever done exactly what James describes in 2:15–17, but have you ever committed a similar sin? Those who do nothing for the poor are just as guilty as those who intentionally oppress others. James' ideas about true religion in 1:27 are related to this.

_____

_____

_____

_____

_____

How can you get involved in helping the poor? What does God want you to do personally?

_____

_____

_____

_____

What does God want the community of believers that you're a part of to do? What are the action items on God's agenda for your life?

_____

_____

_____

_____

"SHOW ME YOUR FAITH"

Pray that God would teach you what it really means to be faithful.

Read James 2:1–20. Reflect on James 2:18–20.

Today, we are faced with the same problems that James dealt with nearly two millennia ago: During the "seeker" movement, droves of people accepted Christ, but many did not accept His lordship over their lives. This problem is what James combats in 2:18—it's ancient and common. It's the unfortunate side of good, convincing preaching, when that preaching is not coupled with discipleship.

What type of works should we practice (1:27; 2:1–17)?

In Matthew 7:15–20, Jesus articulates His view of acting according to faith. Although Jesus is specifically discussing prophets, His view applies to all who believe. How should this inform our understanding of James 2:18–20?

Read Romans 6. Paul's view aligns with James'. How does Paul combat the claim that faith gives us liberty to sin? What type of liberty should we embrace instead (Jas 2:12; see Lesson 4)?

_____

_____

_____

_____

Our faith must extend beyond an intellectual pursuit; otherwise, it is not faith at all. What contrast does James make to affirm this point? What does this contrast demonstrate (2:18)?

_____

_____

_____

_____

What is the result of the rhetorical question in 2:20? How does James characterize faith apart from actions?

_____

_____

_____

_____

In what ways does your faith align with the view James argues for, and in what ways does it differ? What should you be praying about?

_____

_____

_____

GOD'S FRIEND

Pray that the Spirit would reveal to you what it means to be God's friend.

Read James 2:1–24. Reflect on verses 2:21–24.

James 2:21–24 is referencing the Genesis narrative. Read Genesis 17:1–2. What did God ask of Abraham?

_____

_____

_____

_____

What type of law was Abraham called to live by (see Jas 2:12 and Lesson 4)? Also read Genesis 16:1–2. How would Abraham have felt about a son from his proper wife?

_____

_____

_____

_____

Read the rest of Genesis 17. What promise was the birth of Isaac linked to? How did Abraham understand faith (Jas 2:21–22)?

_____

_____

_____

_____

Paul and James both use the term "justified" to describe Abraham (Jas 2:21; Rom 4:1–12). James means that Abraham had a "right" (a "just" or "proper") relationship with God, as shown by his response to God. Abraham is the ideal example of how faith is connected to action. Paul emphasizes that it was Abraham's faith that spurred him on to action (in Abraham's case, circumcision)—thus justifying him (making him right or proper) before God.

James and Paul are essentially making the same point, but they emphasize different aspects: Paul is concerned with the choice that Abraham made, and James is concerned with the actions that resulted from that choice. The two are connected, and both authors acknowledge that (see Jas 2:22; Rom 4:11; Lesson 6).

Paul emphasizes the decision process (the initial faith) because his audience is struggling with affirming the Law over Christ (Rom 3:21–31, especially 3:31). James focuses on actions (faith in action) because his audience is failing to combine their initial faith with their subsequent decisions. For Paul, it's all about the law of faith in Christ (Rom 3:31); James calls this the law of liberty (2:12). Both Paul and James consider actions essential (Jas 1:22–25; Rom 6:1–3).

God only gave Abraham a basic law (Gen 17:1–2). This law, coupled with morals and ethics (common wisdom)—and God's guidance and intervention—helped him make the correct decisions. Sometimes Abraham made the wrong decisions, but ultimately he chose faith (Gen 15:6; Jas 2:23).

Read Genesis 22. What does this story tell us about Abraham's relationship with God? What was he willing to give up, and why (Gen 17:15–21; Jas 2:21–24)?

_____

_____

_____

What steps does God want you to take? How are faith and works connected? How does their connection affect your life?

_____

_____

_____

A DIFFERENT ROUTE?

Pray that God would reveal to you His plans for your life.

Read James 2:1–26. Reflect on verses 2:25–26.

Read Joshua 2 and 6:17. What does the story of Rahab show us about faith and acting on it (Jas 2:25)?

_____

_____

_____

_____

Consider the analogy in James 2:26 and its implications for the way you live out your faith. Write down three ways your faith is currently "dead." Ask someone who you trust to pray with you about these three things. As you pray, meditate upon how your actions can positively affect the lives of others.

_____

_____

_____

_____

Spend the rest of the time you would usually spend studying James to ask God for guidance and wisdom. Ask Him to show you what changes you need to make and what actions you need to take.

CONCLUSION

Many people throughout our world desperately need help. We can't expect people to receive salvation who are struggling from starvation (Jas 2:14–17).

We need to reject the convenience store faith that has become rampant in many of our churches. Christ didn't intend following Him to be easy; He intended for Christ followers to change the world. We have an opportunity. What we do with that opportunity is our decision, but our world will be a morose place if we ignore Christ's call.

Going out of our way for others is how we follow Christ. Making difficult decisions is part of walking with Christ. When we sacrifice ourselves, we respect the God who sacrificed His son. Faith is about action, not consumption. When we as Christians turn our attention to self-sacrifice, we will finally have a faith worth marketing. Simply the gospel could change everything.

JAMES 3

The higher you rise, the easier it is to fall, as any political campaign demonstrates. Accusations can tarnish the reputations of public figures, sometimes blighting them out altogether. Some can't bear the scrutiny and bow out of the race early.

Although James would have bristled at the scandal-loving aspects of modern media, he would have embraced leaders being held accountable in the public eye. James offers practical and simple accountability advice for leaders or teachers, noting the difficulties they face when trying to master self-discipline. Anyone who desires to lead or teach, whether subtly by small decisions or publicly by instructing others, can grow by applying James' understanding of the gospel.

QUESTIONS

 Pray that the Holy Spirit would reveal the questions He wants you to ask yourself and Him.

 Read the entire letter of James aloud in one sitting.

Engaging more that one sense helps us learn and remember. When we use both reading (sight) and reading aloud (hearing), we are more likely to recall God's Word later. As you read the biblical text, make a list of the questions James asks. These questions are rhetorical; they are meant to make us contemplate a principle.

The book of James is very similar to the Wisdom literature of the Old Testament, like Proverbs or Ecclesiastes. The thoughts are pithy, and the implications and applications are far-reaching, affecting all of our relationships.

Next to each rhetorical question, note two implications or applications. Pick a question to contemplate and reflect on it in prayer. Ask God to use the words of James to make you more like Jesus. Also, consider sharing the question with your online social network, family, friends and church—perhaps it will affect others as well.

SO YOU THINK YOU CAN TEACH?

Pray that God would show you whether you're called to teach others and (if so) how.

Read James 1:1–3:18. Reflect on verses 3:1–2.

Why should only a few become teachers?

_____

_____

_____

By "judgment," James means that God holds teachers to a different standard than other people—God expects more from them because they could potentially lead someone away from Christ (see Mark 9:42–50). Teaching and leading are related: All teachers are leaders. And leaders are biblically held to the same standards (i.e., prophets, apostles, elders and deacons are all required to meet set criteria outlined in other biblical passages).

What are the criteria of a "perfect" (whole or complete) person (3:2)?

_____

_____

_____

_____

Like the book of Proverbs, James articulates principles that are practically impossible to meet. He wants to convince people they cannot meet God's standards, that they do need His grace, and that they should respond to His call to be more like Him. God wants people to be humble in spirit and gesture.

We all teach in some form or another. How should teachers respond to this high calling? Should some choose not to teach because of it?

_____

_____

_____

What does James' advice suggest about your approach to teaching? How should your approach change, and how should it remain the same?

_____

_____

_____

BITS, RIDERS, RUDDERS AND CAPTAINS

Pray that God would show the ways your speech needs to change.

Read James 1:5–3:6. Reflect on verses 3:3–4.

In verse 3:3, James elaborates on his thoughts in 3:1–2. By way of analogy, what does James say guides everything we do (3:3)?

_____

_____

_____

By extension of the analogy (3:4), what happens when we don't watch how we speak? Is James referencing merely the type of words we use—vulgar or polite, kind or cruel?

_____

_____

_____

_____

What does the way you speak say about your relationship with others and your view of God? What effect does your speech have on each part of your life?

_____

_____

_____

_____

Based on your reading of this passage, what habits would God like you to change?

_____

_____

_____

_____

MIXING METAPHORS WITH MORE METAPHORS

Pray that Christ would reveal how you can be more diligent about following Him.

Read James 3:1–12. Reflect on verses 3:5–12.

James 3:5 explains the analogies employed in 3:3–4 and then proceeds to mix the metaphors with others. In what ways does the tongue boast? What aspect of the tongue does James emphasize and why? Note the contrasts between the beginning and end of the first sentence in 3:5.

_____

_____

_____

What type of negative power does the tongue have (3:5–6)? In contrast, what good can our speech do?

_____

_____

_____

James intentionally uses hyperbole in 3:6–8. What would happen if we could learn to use our speech entirely for good? How can we learn this discipline?

_____

_____

_____

_____

Why is James' idea especially significant for teachers (3:1–2)?

_____

_____

_____

In James 3:9, by evoking imagery of the "likeness of God," James alludes to ideas from Genesis 1:26–27. Why would he select this terminology? How do we bless God? How do we curse others?

_____

_____

_____

What actions do we take that result in both blessing and cursing? What actions can we take to prevent cursing others?

_____

_____

_____

By employing yet another metaphor, James shows what happens when we fail to follow God's guidance concerning our speech. How do people view teachers who act according to James' analogy?

_____

_____

_____

James' words have implications for all of us. What are four practical ways you can improve the way you speak to others so you can further Christ's message?

_____

_____

_____

Has your recent speech negatively affected your relationships? If so, how can you go about mending those relationships?

_____

_____

_____

BLESSED ARE THE HUMBLE, FOR THEY WILL INHERIT WISDOM

Pray that the Spirit would teach you about humility.

Read James 3:1–18. Reflect on verses 3:13.

How do we know that a person is wise?

_____

_____

_____

In what ways does James 3 reflect the theology articulated in Proverbs 15:32–16:7? How does it explain the connection between wisdom and humility?

_____

_____

_____

_____

Why does someone have to be humble to be wise, and in what ways does being wise articulate humility?

_____

_____

_____

_____

Do you know people who are wise but arrogant? If so, do you think those people are actually reflecting wisdom, or simply knowledge?

_____

_____

_____

How do we receive wisdom (1:5–8)? In what ways is 1:5–8 connected to what we learned in studies 18 and 19?

_____

_____

_____

In what ways are you currently acting unwisely or arrogantly? What are some ways you can change that action? What will be the effect of doing so?

_____

_____

_____

FLAWS ON THE MEND

Pray that God would give you the wisdom to see your own flaws.

Read James 3:13–18. Reflect on James 3:14–16.

James 3:14–16, like this entire passage, is cast in light of how teachers and leaders should act. Considering this, what is the danger of "bitter jealousy" and "selfish ambition"?

_____

_____

_____

_____

In what ways can leaders "tell lies against the truth" (the good news of Jesus)? How do we identify the "unspiritual" or the "demonic" (3:15)? With what does James juxtapose this phrase?

_____

_____

_____

_____

What happens when someone seeks earthly wisdom instead of God's wisdom (3:16)? In what ways is the effect obvious?

_____

_____

_____

_____

Note the spiritual implications of seeking earthly wisdom in light of God's will to make the world orderly, including our lives, and thereby empower us to bring order to the chaos of other people's lives and to our world. We know this theme is part of the backdrop of James, because 3:9 refers to the passage where God notes that He has created people in His likeness (Gen 1:26–27) — the pinnacle of His creative work, meant to vanquish chaos and make the world orderly.

In what ways are you demonstrating "bitter jealousy" and "selfish ambition"? Ask God to help you identify ways you show these attributes, the relationships in which you show them and how to change your actions to reflect wisdom.

WISDOM'S TEST

Pray that the Spirit would show you the attributes of wisdom and how to incorporate them into your life.

Read James 3:13-18. Reflect on verse 3:17.

James 3:17 offers an alternative to being filled with "bitter jealousy" and "selfish ambition" (3:14–16). Where does wisdom come from?

_____

_____

_____

How does a wise person act? Look up each of these attributes using Bible software, Biblia.com or a concordance. (If you're studying in a group, have each person look up one of the six attributes.)

_____

_____

_____

_____

What particular thing do the wise abstain from? How does this articulate the value of a "perfect" (whole or complete) teacher (3:1)? What type of feelings do we have about leaders who don't exemplify this attribute?

_____

_____

_____

_____

Which of these attributes do you exemplify most, and how can you enhance the others?

_____

_____

_____

REFLECTING GOD'S IMAGE

Pray that God would reveal to you His plans for your life.

Read James 3:1–18. Reflect on verse 3:18

Look up "righteousness" in a concordance or search using Bible software or Biblia.com. How do you define righteousness based on the contexts in which it is used? How does righteousness create spiritual fruit (good things and outcomes)?

_____

_____

_____

How do peaceful people receive a peaceful message? By contrast, how do disgruntled people or conflict-mongers receive a peaceful message?

_____

_____

_____

_____

Being made in God's likeness (Jas 3:9; Gen 1:26–27) is directly connected to the idea of being a "son of God" (Matt 5:9). Being a son of God means being part of God's family (that is, being like Him). What does Jesus say about peacemakers in Matthew 5:9?

_____

_____

_____

How is our wisdom, or lack thereof, connected to our ability to reflect God's image to others (Jas 1:5–8; 3:14–17)? Why are all who teach especially called to this standard (3:1–2)?

_____

_____

_____

Do your actions demonstrate that you love peace, or that you prefer to be right?

_____

_____

_____

What are some simple and practical ways you can you change your actions so they better articulate the values of Christ? Share these with a friend and ask them to pray for you.

_____

_____

_____

CONCLUSION

Every time we declare we are Christ-followers, we represent Him. Whether you are the leader of a large Christian movement or the only Christian in your workplace, mistakes can be fatal to your proclamation of the gospel message.

Nearly every day, we have the chance to drive someone closer to Jesus or farther away. By simply choosing to be peacemakers, determining to seek wisdom, and working to live rightly for Christ's sake—by demonstrating spiritual fruit—we can draw people to Him. Like the old hymn goes, "They will know we are Christians by our love"; they will also know we are Christians because we live differently. We live with purpose. Jesus' simple gospel, proclaimed through the empowerment of His wisdom, is our means.

JAMES 4:1–5:6

Often, the stuff you think will be a problem usually isn't and the things you don't think twice about are the problem. This is equally applicable to our relationship with God: The more we communicate with Him, the more likely we are to acknowledge hidden problems. And when we acknowledge the real problems, current concerns rightly drift into subconsciousness. Often, the real problems are obvious to others but not to us, affecting those relationships in ways we didn't realize. So ask for God's grace and others' forgiveness, then correct as needed.

Like the stock market, returns on relationships are proportionate to what you're willing to risk. You don't see large gains unless you're willing to go big on a possible flop. The difference, though, is that God is the one measuring success, and you may not see your rewards in this lifetime. The book of James frames four major spiritual issues similarly: living as a Christian when overwhelmed by alternative values, judging others, desiring to succeed and managing wealth. These are areas of potentially hidden problems—and the law of diminishing returns suggests that we could be unaware of astronomical losses in each area. In the next eight studies, we will learn how to identify problems in these areas and how God wants to work in us to solve them. The results will be enriched relationships and improvement in the lives of those around us.

MEANING AMID HYPERBOLE

Pray that God would reveal how James' broad statements apply to you.

Read the entire letter of James aloud in one sitting.

When we regularly read biblical books aloud, we have a higher chance of picking up on the details that relate to the book's overall meaning. The more often you read a book (and hear it), the more likely you are to perceive nuances and connect ideas from one phrase to the next. As you read the book, underline passages that reflect a change in tone. Why does James shift his tone?

_____

_____

_____

James often uses hyperbole to make his points memorable. What are some of his hyperbolic points in chapter four?

_____

_____

_____

Note the points you think he is conveying next to each hyperbole: what's applicable about the point—not just to those who have committed the specific sin he mentions, but to everyone?

_____

_____

_____

_____

How can you apply these points to your walk with Jesus?

_____

_____

_____

_____

THE WAR WITHIN

Pray that the Spirit would reveal ways your relationship with God is misaligned with His will.

Read James 1:1–4:11. Reflect on verses 4:1–6.

What is one of the sources of conflicts among believers (4:1)?

_____

_____

_____

"Members" also evokes the idea that we as believers are at war against our own desires (what our bodies want and what evil prompts us to do). What are some ways to combat this problem? Think about the larger context of James here— as with Lesson 1. Also note that James is primarily speaking in hyperbole in 4:1–6, although some of the sins he lists are relevant to both believers and those yet to accept Christ.

_____

_____

_____

_____

According to the beginning of 4:2, what leads to murder, fighting and quarrelling?

_____

_____

_____

The last phrase in 4:3 evokes James' early thoughts on wisdom and prayer. Why does he make similar statements here, and how has the context and application changed?

_____

_____

_____

Why and how is a desire for godly wisdom misaligned with 4:3?

_____

_____

_____

"The world" is used in 4:4 to reference things opposed to God; it represents evil. James 4:4 is not suggesting that all things in the world are evil or wrong. How does someone become an enemy of God, and what does that look like compared to the Christian framework articulated in 1:18–27, specifically 1:27?

_____

_____

_____

James 4:5 is difficult to translate; it could be suggesting that God's Spirit becomes jealous whenever we desire things outside of His will, or that God longs for His Spirit to completely envelop us—to take over our evil desires and lead us perfectly in His ways. (The citation in 4:5 is of unknown origins.)

James 4:6 cites Proverbs 3:34. Read Proverbs 3:33–35. James often alludes to wisdom traditions like Proverbs to suggest that his argument is self-evident and needs no further explanation—suggesting that it's clearly in God's will. In what ways is Proverbs 3:33–35 self-evident in your experiences?

_____

_____

_____

In what ways have you become metaphorically adulterous? How is your relationship with God misaligned with His actual will? What value sets do you have that God wishes to overcome?

_____

_____

_____

AND HE WILL DRAW NEAR TO YOU

Pray that God would show you what it means to draw near to Him.

Read James 1:5–4:10. Reflect on verses 4:7–10.

How do we subject ourselves to God (4:7)? What are some basic steps for doing so?

_____

_____

_____

_____

What does James' understanding of the nature of temptation, as articulated in 1:12–18, suggest about his understanding of temptation in 4:7?

_____

_____

_____

_____

How can we flee from the devil, temptation and evil? What does that look like from a practical standpoint?

_____

_____

_____

_____

In the second half of 4:8, James references cleansing rituals from the Old Testament, like Leviticus 16:19. The passage details how the altar should be cleansed so that a goat could be offered for the people's sin. James also alludes to purity rituals, like the one described in Leviticus 8:15, where Moses purifies the altar for a sin offering. Both the phrases "cleanse hands, sinners" and "purify hearts, double-minded ones" allude to the problem of sin and other problems involved with coming before God in ancient Israel (e.g., Lev 12:4–6; 14:2–8).

James is pointing out that the people are subjecting themselves to temptation and thus sin, rather than subjecting themselves to God—and by implication, the freedom Christ has given them. This is why James tells the people in 4:9 to lament, mourn, weep and be gloomy: They are joyful in their evil. The first halves of 4:8 and 4:10 are bookends to this argument. In light of this, what do these two phrases mean?

_____

_____

_____

What habits can you change to subject yourself to Christ? (God's goal is that we would always be subjected to Christ.)

_____

_____

_____

AN ALTERNATIVE

Pray that the Spirit would help you identify how you judge others.

Read James 4:1–12. Reflect on verses 4:11–12.

What's at stake when we "speak evil" of others (4:11)?

_____

_____

_____

_____

The "law" that James references in 4:11 is the "royal law"—defined in 2:8 through a quote of Leviticus 19:18—which itself is related to the "law of liberty" defined in James 1:25–27. With this understanding in mind, what is the application of the second half of 4:11?

_____

_____

_____

_____

What does it mean to only be a "judge" of the law, considering the larger context of James' ideas about the law?

_____

_____

_____

_____

Why is God opposed to people judging others (4:12)? What role do we attempt to play when doing so?

_____

_____

_____

Rather than judging, what's our obligation to other people (1:27)?

_____

_____

_____

In what ways do you currently judge others? How can you temper a judging spirit?

_____

_____

_____

A BOLD DESIRE

Pray that God would help you to focus on His goals, not your own.

Read James 4:1–15. Reflect on verses 4:13–15.

What's wrong with the type of people that James describes in 4:13 (see 4:14)? What can we be unaware of, and how can it hinder our plans (4:14)? How can our plans hinder God's plans?

_____

_____

_____

_____

What clause in 4:15 should all our life plans depend on?

_____

_____

_____

_____

The underlying concept of James is the realization that God's view of success and joy is not the same as ours. Pray about your current plans: In what ways are they causing you to sin? How are these plans connected to moments of temptation? (Also consider this in light of what we learned in Lesson 3.)

_____

_____

_____

_____

A HIDDEN DANGER

Pray that God would teach you His ideas about humility.

Read James 4:1–17. Reflect on verses 4:16–17.

How would you describe the type of arrogance James has in view (4:16)? Consider this in light of 4:13–15 and Lesson 5.

_____

_____

_____

_____

Apathy is a sin that is often overlooked—whether it's apathy toward God's plans for our lives or apathy toward others. This is the issue at stake in 4:17. How does ambition hinder doing good for others (compare 1:27)? How can the royal law be a guiding principle in these circumstances (2:8; see Lesson 4)?

_____

_____

_____

_____

What are two ways that your confidence in your plans, or your lack of acknowledgment of God's plans, are making you arrogant?

_____

_____

_____

_____

What are approaches that would not just eliminate the perpetual sin problem, but provide an alternative?

_____

_____

_____

What are two recent things you didn't do, even though you knew God was asking you to do them? How will you respond next time?

_____

_____

_____

How has desire for success encouraged your apathy, and what can you do instead?

_____

_____

_____

THE WEALTH PARADOX

Pray that God will help you develop a right attitude toward wealth.

Read James 4:1–5:3. Reflect on verses 5:1–3.

What type of problems can wealth create? What "miseries" can it bring? Consider this based on your own experience or others' experiences while reflecting on 5:2–3.

_____

_____

_____

It's not wealth itself that is the problem, but the way that it is appropriated and used. How does James suggest that wealth should be used (1:27)? Read Acts 2:42–27. What was the first church's response to wealth?

_____

_____

_____

With poverty in nearly all communities in the world and the ever-increasing problem of extreme global poverty (25,000 children under age 5 die daily from poverty-related causes), how can churches today mobilize to deal with these problems? How can your church tackle these issues? What can you personally do? What do James 1:27 and 5:1–3 suggest you do?

_____

_____

_____

_____

"These last days" in 5:3 is a reference to the time between Christ's ascension into heaven after His resurrection and the time before He will come again to earth. Wealth is of no value when the future currency of the world will be relationships, especially our relationship with Christ. Wealth is a paradox that can be used for the good described in Acts 2:42–27 and James 1:27, but simultaneously can hinder our relationship with God.

What happens to wealth over time? And what is the effect of wealth on a believer if they don't use it to help others (5:3)?

_____

_____

_____

In what ways does God wish for you to change the way you use your wealth?

_____

_____

_____

THE POWER PARADOX

Pray that God would show you how to use your influence for good.

Read James 4:1–5:6. Reflect on verses 5:4–6.

James uses an ancient analogy that is equally relevant for the modern employer in 5:4. What happens when we don't pay someone their wages or pay them fairly?

_____

_____

_____

_____

What does the metaphor "fattened your hearts in the day of slaughter" mean contextually (5:5)?

_____

_____

_____

_____

How can we metaphorically "murder" the righteous person (5:6)? How does what we learned in Lesson 4 expound on this point?

_____

_____

_____

_____

Lord Acton's quote, "Power tends to corrupt, and absolute power corrupts absolutely," is illustrated here in James. How do 5:1–3 (as discussed in the previous lesson) and 5:4–6 act as precursors to Lord Acton's quote?

_____

_____

_____

The paradox of power is that it tends to make people delusional—believing that what is evil is right and what is right is unnecessary empathy—when power is meant to give them opportunities to help the hurting (Jas 1:27). Apathy is one of the great enemies of Christianity. We all have a sphere of influence, and thus we all have some form of power. How would God like you to alter the way you use your power? List four ways and pray about them. Also ask someone else you trust to pray about them.

_____

_____

_____

_____

CONCLUSION

Every time we invest in the currencies of this world—whether through feelings of supremacy, condoning sin, selfish ambition, misplaced self-esteem, belief in wealth or passion for power—we sacrifice part of God's glorious vision for our lives. These issues, as addressed in James 4:1–5:6, can hinder our relationship with Christ and others.

Simply, the gospel is the alternative—a life lived for God and others. And the alternative is beautiful: a world actually changed, in these last days, by those who claim to believe in something better. It's something worth exchanging with the currencies of this age since lives depend on the choices we make. There is something incredible about the idea that we're all connected and in need of God's grace and the graciousness of others. That's what the kingdom of God is all about. We each have a choice to make.

JAMES 5:7–20

If patience is a virtue, few of us are virtuous. If asked, many would have to pause to recall the last time we wished for more patience. We live in the "now" age; everything is fast and we always want faster. But that's not an excuse. The red exclamation point that used to mark urgency in the email inbox has lost its meaning and become more of a nuisance. Have you ever found yourself writing in e-mails "this isn't urgent" because it's the standard to assume otherwise? Some of this certainly comes down to our own idiosyncrasies and flaws, but most of us can relate. Yet James insists we need patience.

We're told in Psalm 90:4 that to God, a thousand years is like "a watch in the night." Although at times we feel like we're waiting for a thousand years, in the course of human history our entire lives are fleeting (Eccl 8:8). Nonetheless, they have incredible meaning not just for the now, but for the future. This is one reason why James insists on patience, but as we will explore in these next eight studies, he is also concerned about something bigger: Jesus is coming.

SOCIAL CHANGE

Pray that the Spirit would reveal to you how you can help those who are struggling or suffering.

Read the entire letter of James aloud in one sitting.

Since reading aloud requires us to use two of our senses, it enhances the contemplation process. The longer we spend reflecting on the meaning of each phrase in relation to the previous phrases (as well as each section in regard to the previous sections), the deeper the meaning of the book becomes for us, and the more prolonged its effects are upon our lives. If the book of James were a story, what would be the prologue, the major conflict, the minor conflicts and the resolution?

_____

_____

_____

What conflicts does James address that are conflicts in your own life? What are the resolutions?

_____

_____

_____

How does James 5:7–20 connect to the rest of the book? In light of the rest of James' points, why does he make these statements?

_____

_____

_____

Why are the last lines of James crucial to how we apply the entire book?

_____

_____

_____

James is a social book; it's about how we interact with Christ and others. It's about what we're willing to give to Jesus, and the decision to be obedient when God calls us to give to others. It's about learning to love fully and care for those in need. How does your life align with this message? In what ways are you misaligned with God's plans?

_____

_____

_____

THE FARMER WAITS

Pray that God would teach you patience.

Read James 1:1–5:8. Reflect on verses 5:7–8.

When we repetitively reflect on a biblical book, we see shades of meaning that we may not have seen before.

Why does James use the example of a farmer to illustrate the principle of patience (5:7)?

_____

_____

_____

_____

How does James' example symbolize spirituality, both in terms of our relationship with Jesus and in regard to others' relationships (or lack thereof) with Christ?

_____

_____

_____

What does the "coming of the Lord" have to do with patience (5:8)? Is it merely about awaiting His arrival, or is it also relevant to how we decide to act now?

_____

_____

_____

_____

Read 2 Peter 3:8–13. It seems odd that James would act like Jesus' coming is imminent though it hasn't happened yet. What is the explanation for this, according to 2 Peter 3:8–13?

_____

_____

_____

Why is Jesus' second coming to earth at the center of the Christian faith? What are we to do in expectation of His coming?

_____

_____

_____

What does patience look like for a Christian? How does James' idea of patience compare or contrast with your own?

_____

_____

_____

How can you correct your impatience?

_____

_____

_____

What are some tangible things that you can pray about? What intangible things (like what you feel or think) can you pray about?

_____

_____

_____

NO ONE LIKES A WHINER

Pray that God would reveal to you what endurance looks like in a godly community.

Read James 1:5–5:10. Reflect on verses 5:9–10.

Why is complaining against others detrimental to Christ's work among us (5:9)?

_____

_____

_____

What happens to us when we complain against others? What risks do we run (5:9)?

_____

_____

_____

James discusses the example of the prophets in 5:10 because the prophets had ample opportunity to create strife among themselves and others. Yet they decided not to, even when they disagreed; the prophets chose unity for the sake of the greater good of God's work.

Multiple prophets were often present in one king's court, country or region. Similarly, when God's people were divided, the opposing powers of Judah and Israel each had their own prophets. Allegiance to a nation, or a desire for recognition, could have divided God's people further, and this would have made His will more difficult for them to hear and receive.

It was the duty of prophets, and still is for Christians, to seek the fulfillment of God's will over (and often against) personal gain or feelings. This is not to say that peace is always the right answer, but it certainly is when both parties have God's will in mind.

In what ways are you creating strife? How can you bring peace instead?

_____

_____

_____

In what ways is God calling you to persevere (5:10)?

_____

_____

_____

LESSON 4

ENDURANCE IS ONLY LEARNED THE HARD WAY

Pray that Christ would show you how your commitments are helping or impeding your relationship with him.

Read James 4:1–5:12. Reflect on verses 5:11–12.

James 5:11 tells us that Job is an example of someone with endurance. Read Job 1:1–2:10; 42:1–6; and 42:10–17. What did Job learn during the process of his suffering?

_____

_____

_____

_____

What message does God have for you in the story of Job? What does Job's story teach us about God (Jas 5:11)?

_____

_____

_____

_____

Why should we view people who have endured hardship as blessed (5:11)?

_____

_____

_____

In light of the story of Job and what we know about people's ability to keep their word (in general), why does James advise against making an oath (or swearing by anything; 5:12)? How does making such an oath affect your openness to God's ability to work in your life?

_____

_____

_____

What do you currently make oaths about? What should you do instead, and why (5:12)?

_____

_____

_____

BEYOND A MEDICAL DIAGNOSIS

 Pray that God would show you the reason for sickness and pain and the ultimate cure.

 Read James 5:1–15. Reflect on verses 5:13–15.

"Suffering misfortune" in James 5:13 probably is a reference to persecution because of faith in Christ; two other occurrences of this word in the New Testament also allude to this (2 Tim 2:9; 4:5). Broadly, this phrase can be applied to enduring hardship for following God's calling. James says we should pray when these things occur; we should ask God to give us guidance.

There are times when we're called to hardship for the sake of spreading the good news of Jesus. Paul said that his suffering in prison was in the service of the gospel: It verified the authenticity of his commitment to Christ, gave him the chance to initiate letters about Jesus (which became biblical books) and provided him with the opportunity to minister to other prisoners (Acts 16:25–34). His suffering also taught him what it was like for Christ to suffer, helping him grow closer to Jesus.

What should we do when God brings joy into our lives (5:13)?

_____

_____

_____

_____

_____

_____

Our responses to hardship and joy have the same object: God. We're often better at praying for God to intercede than thanking Him for His current intercession. What can we do to establish an attitude of admiration and thankfulness toward God?

_____

_____

_____

_____

What should people do when they have an illness (5:14)? Do people in your church react the way James recommends? Do you react this way?

_____

_____

_____

_____

How can you be an instrument of change to help the sick? How must we pray for the ill (5:15)? (Anointing oil symbolizes God's decision to intercede and/or the request that He mark a person set apart for His work. Thus, the miracles that God performs should be used for glorifying Him.)

_____

_____

_____

_____

In 5:15, James uses the word "save" in the sense that by interceding, the person acts as God's vehicle for deliverance. Requesting that God perform a miracle is a way of presenting a person before God and, consequently, giving Him the opportunity to show His glory through that person. What's so powerful about this idea is that God uses people for His saving work, even though we are not capable of doing this work on our own.

James relates sickness to sin (5:15), a common theme in the Gospels. At times, sickness is related to disobedience against God and others and thus is not merely medical (Psa 107:17; Mic 6:13). In our scientific mindset, we often forget that everything is related to spirituality. Some conditions are purely medical and completely unrelated to sin, but at times, illnesses *are* related to sin. In this regard, how should you change your approach to helping the sick? How should you change your approach to your own ailments?

_____

_____

_____

_____

How should you go about moving past sin in your life and accepting the grace that Jesus offers you?

_____

_____

_____

_____

WHEN IT RAINS

Pray that God would show you why we pray.

Read James 5:1–18. Reflect on verses 5:16–18.

Reflecting on what we learned in week five, why is it important to confess our sins to others (5:16)? What are the dangers of not doing so?

_____

_____

_____

We are made righteous by Christ's sacrifice for us, not by our own merit (Rom 3:23–24); James is referring to something else at the end of 5:16 when he discusses righteousness. James means that people are currently in right standing in their relationship with God in the sense that they are open to Him and others about their sins and struggles; they are battling against them with the help of their Christian community.

Those who are following God intently are able to do much more than those who are not. The righteousness that we are granted because of Christ's sacrifice should be used to help others become free in Him, not as an excuse to do what we would like.

Read 1 Kings 16:29–17:7; 18:41–46. Why did Elijah pray against rain and then eventually pray *for* rain (Jas 5:17–18)? Why would James use this example to explain prayer to us?

_____

_____

_____

_____

In what ways do your prayers reflect the fervency of Elijah and how do they not? What can you do to make the necessary changes? (Habits are difficult to change, so think seriously about this.)

_____

_____

_____

LEADING

Pray that the spirit would reveal whom He desires for you to bring back to the truth.

Read James 5:1–20. Reflect on verses 5:19–20.

What should we do when people walk away from the truth of what Jesus has done for them and His plans for their lives? (Note that the term "brothers" in the New Testament can be broadly applied to "brothers and sisters" in most usages, including the one here in Jas 5:19.)

In 5:19, like in 5:15, James uses the word "save" broadly to refer to someone's ability to do God's work. Similarly, "save" is often used in the New Testament to refer to someone being freed from demon possession (see Luke 8:36; Acts 4:9). Those who act on behalf of Jesus can be vehicles of His saving work—not in the sense of justifying people before God, but in the sense of helping them turn from one path toward God's better path; they're a type of deliverer.

Christians are not saviors in the way that Jesus is. Instead, they are vehicles to proclaim His salvation. In this regard, Christians can cover "a great number of sins" (5:20): By helping someone number or name his or her sins, they put that person in a position to easily call out to Christ—the ultimate truth. In this way, people are led into, or back to, Christ's path for their lives. It is our duty to help others find their way toward the grace that God freely offers through Jesus.

Where does the path against God's will lead (5:20)? How can you be an instrument to lead people back into God's path, and how can you allow others to lead you back into God's truth?

_____

_____

_____

_____

_____

TAKING A CUE FROM JAMES

Pray that the Spirit would show you what needs to change in your life and how to change it.

Read the entire book of James in one sitting.

In light of the book of James, reflect on what you should change in your life. How is God working in you and speaking to you? What is your response to the prompting of His Spirit?

_____

_____

_____

_____

Take the rest of the time you would usually spend studying the book of James to pray about the concepts it presents. Pray for God's will for your life and for those who need to hear Jesus' message or return to it.

_____

_____

_____

_____

CONCLUSION

James' picture of a patient Christian is not someone sitting down waiting for Jesus to lift him or her out of this world. Instead, it's someone building a path toward Christ. We build this path by being compassionate. In the process of building, we must remove the mental, physical and spiritual barriers between people and God. We must make it easy for them to seek Jesus back by seeing Him in us.

We learn patience through our longing to be with Christ. However, being patient doesn't mean complacency. When James speaks about being patient, he doesn't leave out the actions we should take while waiting for Jesus to come again. We should be patient in the sense that we wait until we know where and how He wants us to build His path before acting.

We should also pray because the time of grace between now and His coming again is limited. We only have so long to help others get on the right path; every minute is one less to share the good news. And every time we turn away is a moment lost for God's kingdom.

The Christian story is not meant to be one of people searching for comfort. It's a story of people who have already found affirmation in Christ, who chose us— and people who are now working to show others the elegance of that story. May you be fervently patient.